the One Tiger

the One Tiger

Gill Davies

The One Tiger

First published 2008

© SeaSquirt Books 2008

Ty Ganol Rhodiad y Brenin St Davids Pembrokeshire Wales

ISBN 978-1-905470-23-5

British Library CIP Data

A catalogue record of this book is available from the British Library

Series concept David Hughes

Written by Gill Davies

Photographs by Rodney Griffiths and others

Printed and bound by Gomer Press Limited, Wales

Contents

About the paper on which *The One Tiger* is printed

Paper is made from fibres that are found in the cell walls of all plants. The fibres mainly come from plant sources such as wood, bamboo, cotton, jute, or even rice. However, wood from trees is the main source of fibres used in paper making. A mixture of water and fibres is filtered through a screen to make a sheet of paper. When the paper is dried chemical bonds form to give the paper its strength.

The One Tiger is printed on paper in which at least 75% of the fibre has been recycled. This means it comes from materials that have been used before.

The main sources from which recycled paper is made are newspapers, magazines, directories, leaflets, office and computer paper, cardboard from boxes and packing, mixed or coloured papers.

 NAPM approved
recycled product

This book is printed on Revive Matt from the Robert Horne Group.
It contains at least 75% de-inked post-consumer waste fibre.

The One Tiger

Tigers are among the most majestic and dramatic creatures on this earth - with a roar can be heard up to three kilometres (two miles) away. Today they are vanishing - at an astonishingly fast rate.

As tree clearance moves on apace and cities and farms spread ever further into jungle terrain, hunting and forest destruction have reduced tiger populations from hundreds of thousands a century ago to far less than 5,000 now. The tiger is in crisis.

In The One Tiger, the verses take us into the world of this magnificent creature - through his dreams and his roars, through his vision of the jungle environment, we discover just a little of what being a tiger means and just how much there is to lose.

Gill Davies

An emerald world

The One Tiger roars!
And as the splendid, beautiful One Tiger roars . . .

Glossy emerald leaves quiver and rattle,
nearby parrots cease their jungle tittle-tattle;
lizards rush up branches covered in vines
where orchids and mosses intertwine,
and a march of ants busy-busy flows
towards beetles gleaming where undergrowth grows.
An elephant trumpets as the One Tiger calls,
tossing great ears and standing tall
next to a mighty roaring waterfall,
where butterflies flit and peacocks call:
For when One Tiger speaks, the animals listen
as snakes stop mid-coil and bright skins glisten . . .

**For the jungle will listen and pause
listen and pause when the One Tiger roars!**

A dream of running

The One Tiger roars . . .

As the One Tiger roars with all his might
monkeys scatter in the trees; cranes take flight:
But now One Tiger is dreaming in the daytime heat . . .
dreaming of running with pounding feet,
that throb with a rhythmic thumping beat,
where emerald grass and blue sky meet.

His tail is taut as he bounds on paws
that shield beneath them terrible claws
as terrible as his ferocious jaws . . .
Jaws that can make even crocodiles pause;
for the jungle listens when One Tiger roars
from its highest tree to its swampiest shores.

The One Tiger roars with ferocious jaws
and the jungle listens when One Tiger roars . . .

Mother and cubs

The One Tiger dreams . . .

He dreams as his ears and whiskers twitch:
his black stripes ripple in a pattern laid rich
across a golden-orange glowing fur.
Tiger's roar now softens and becomes a purr
as he dreams of his mate, so strong and lithe
and how, as a pair, they move and glide.

He dreams of his cubs that play and growl,
concentrating with young but fearsome scowls
as the cubs practise a pounce, and roll and fight,
ever under their mother's watchful sight.
The cubs sleep as she prowls in the starry night
with the moon high above and bats in flight.

**One Tiger dreams she is here beside,
here beside, with her rippling glide.**

Sky and snow

Tiger dreams of the sky . . .

Now the tiger dreams of climbing high
Up over stony crags to reach an azure sky.
The rugged rocks make a sharp-edged throne
as he surveys his world up there alone.
His sharp eyes sweep the jungle below
As he dreams of his cousins and cold, cold snow.

Siberian tigers have paler stripes and fur
and live where snow falls most of the year.
These, the largest of all cats everywhere,
hunt elk and deer, lynx and bear.
They hide among birch trees and oak and pine
but only very few survive as their numbers decline.

**Tiger dreams of the snow, the snow-flaked snow
tumbling soft in a moonlit glow.**

Mirror of water

The One Tiger now dreams a different scene . . .

For the One Tiger here knows a different scene . . .
where the sun blazes down and the world is green,
where the crocodile shares his waterside space
with his snapping, toothsome knobbly face,
where leopards prowl with their spots ablaze
and crumpled rhinos grunt and graze.

Then the One Tiger yawns and unfurls his tongue
as he recalls his thirst when the sun burns strong;
how he seeks cool pools to soothe his hot, hot skin,
how their mirrored stillness takes him in.
how fit he feels when he swims along,
no river too wide nor current too strong.

**Swim along, swim along,
no river too wide, no current too strong.**

17

Awake

Now the One Tiger wakes . . .

The One Tiger stirs, wakes, washes his paws,
staring and thinking, a moment of pause,
then his busy, rasping tongue finds fur and claws
as he sweeps and nibbles with delicate jaws.
Soon his coat is gleaming, his grooming is done.
Will he sleep again - or wake and run?

Will he stalk between the dense, tall waving reeds
and see where the long-legged stilt birds feed?
Will he visit the edge of the mangrove shores
where bright crabs scuttle and wave their claws?
He might tiptoe along a grassy path
as snakes slither off and hyenas laugh?

Softly tread . . . what's ahead?
Sniff the scents others shed.

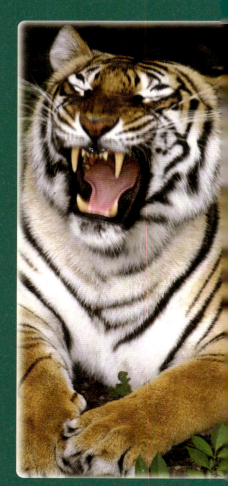

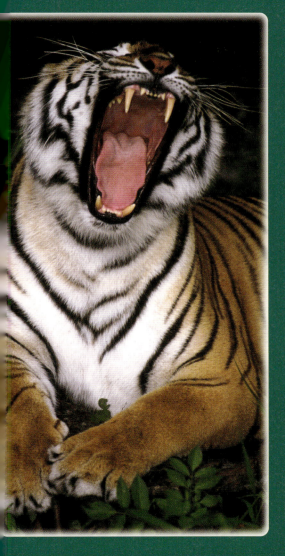

Prowl, watch, wait

One tiger prowls . . .

He may prowl through forests with trees set deep
where sunlight shafts pour slanted and steep
and the canopy above hides the rest of the sky
where sharp-eyed eagles hunt and fly
as the One Tiger's paws step stealthily by
and the humid air seems to breathe and sigh.

He may lie in wait and peep through the trees,
his image blurred by the dripping leaves,
his stripes a disguise that hide his shape,
as the jungle around him silently drapes
a cloak on his shoulders, so he's scarcely there,
only to be seen by the most aware.

A cloak, a mystery, strong disguise
hidden from other prying jungle eyes.

All tigerness aware

The One Tiger stirs . . .

It is time to move. The One Tiger stirs,
A yawn, a short snarl, a couple of purrs.
He is stretching, rediscovering body and strength,
muscles, flanks and stripe-circled length.
Here are whiskers that tingle aside mighty jaws
Here's a tail that swings and paws with claws.

He revels in the stillness, of resting there,
of simply being just a tiger, of all tigerness aware.
But it is time to move, it is time to hunt,
With sharp ears listening and nose out front,
His night eyes are keen, as sharp as an owl
As the tiger prepares for his evening prowl.

He prepares for his prowl with a steely stare,
all senses alert, aroused and aware.

One Tiger is hungry . . .

Will he eat tonight? It is hard to say
for so often his prey escapes away.
One Tiger sniffs the air and looks around
but his ears are disturbed by an ugly sound.
Men are sawing down trees, too close it seems
and the noise often disturbs his waking dreams.

Soon the forests may vanish and turn to dust.
The One Tiger knows life can be unjust:
He must kill to survive; he must kill to eat
and many gentle creatures will serve as his meat
but while nature seeks a balance and each does as it must,
all will be threatened if the jungle is crushed.

All will be threatened as trees crash down,
down to the ground, earth-shuddering down

The Only One

Soon the tiger's domain may be long gone:
Soon the One Tiger may be the Only One . . .
No tigress to visit, no cubs at play,
no future generations to save the day,
to tell of the place the One Tiger knew
where great trees flourished and hornbills flew.

Already tigers in thousands have disappeared.
Species have vanished; no more young can be reared.
All the One Tiger knows is that his own space is less
as forests are cleared to aid 'progress',
to build towns and to farm, where man can live
but on land that is barren and has little to give.

**Little to raise from land so bruised,
snatched from the Tiger; so much to lose.**

"This jungle is beautiful"

The One Tiger roars . . .

As the One Tiger roars with all his might,
he should tell the jungle creatures they need to unite;
they need to fight to survive this terrible plight,
they need to make a stand for their jungle rights,
from tiny bugs scampering on moonlit nights
to the birds that sing in the treetop heights.

"This jungle is beautiful," One Tiger should roar
"We cannot let it vanish from beneath our paws.
We cannot let it be chopped and taken away.
We need it to last so that we can stay.
Once we were hunted and skinned and abused
but the disappearing jungle is even worse news."

So One Tiger roars, a sound now rare
but One Tiger roars, unaware, unaware.

The One Tiger, unaware!

Tiger roars and roars, unaware . . .

The One Tiger roars!
But he really should cry,
as he stares at the world through unblinking eyes
and understands not that his end is nigh.

Will anyone awake and serve his needs?
Will anyone notice and save the trees?
Will the emerald jungle be allowed to remain?
Oh, please, somebody respond to the tiger's pain?

Such a regal creature, such a joy to view,
So strong, so powerful, but vulnerable too.
Unaware, the One Tiger heads this crisis now,
The food chain captain, holding the prow.

The One Tiger roars.
The One Tiger sighs . . .
But One Tiger will vanish
if the only One Tiger dies.

the One

Series of eco-aware books

"If you haven't already been an eco-warrior . . . these may well set that in motion."

The Scotsman - August 2007
Review of plays of the books The One Tree and The One Sea.

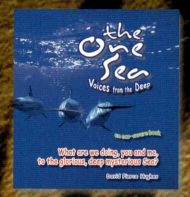

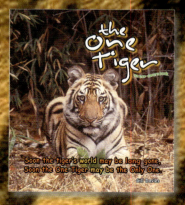

This book was designed and typeset by
Playne Books Limited
Park Court Barn
Trefin
Haverfordwest
Pembrokeshire
SA62 5AU

Photographs on the cover and pages 2 and 3, 6 and 7, 10 and 11, 12 and 13, 14 and 15, 18 and 19, 24, 26 and 27, 28 and 29, 30 and 31 are by **Rodney Griffiths**.

Others are from Playne Books photographic library.